IMAGES
of Rail

PACIFIC ELECTRIC
RED CARS

IMAGES
of Rail

PACIFIC ELECTRIC
RED CARS

Jim Walker

ARCADIA
PUBLISHING

Published by Arcadia Publishing
Charleston, South Carolina

Library of Congress Catalog Card Number: 2006931273

For all general information contact Arcadia Publishing at:
Telephone 843-853-2070
Fax 843-853-0044
E-mail sales@arcadiapublishing.com
For customer service and orders:
Toll-Free 1-888-313-2665

Visit us on the Internet at www.arcadiapublishing.com

*This book is dedicated to the memory of Henry Edwards Huntington,
rail tycoon, developer, and benefactor.*

CONTENTS

ACKNOWLEDGMENTS

The author would like to acknowledge the many organizations and individuals who have provided images, information, advice, and guidance for this project.

Thanks to the Los Angeles County Metropolitan Transportation Authority (LACMTA) and its Dorothy P. Gray Transportation Library and to Matthew Barrett, the library's administrator.

Thanks also to Craig Rasmussen for many images used throughout the book and to P. Allen Copeland and Dave Garcia for historic information. Thanks to Jerry Roberts of Arcadia Publishing for editing help.

Photograph Credits

The bulk of the images in this book are in the LACMTA Dorothy P. Gray Library. Thanks also to Craig Rasmussen for his large contribution of photographs from his substantial Pacific Electric collection. And, finally, thanks to many people who have over the years graciously assisted me in gathering information and images concerning Pacific Electric and other rail lines.

Please note that although the information in this book is well researched, some factual errors may have crept in. I hope that these are at a minimum. Also, comments and opinions are only those of the author.

Jim Walker
Los Angeles, California
July 2006

INTRODUCTION

The history of Southern California in the 20th century is intertwined with the development, growth, and commuters' everyday use of the Pacific Electric Railway. Known by its initials, PE, this great interurban transportation system left an indelible footprint in shaping Southern California. Its tracks and right-of-ways gave many of the transportation corridors that are present today. The PE-linked businesses and families brought relatively safe, cheap, easy, and fast travel to generations of an entire region—even as rutted traces became asphalt highways and gas buggies began to be essential for families.

When thinking of the PE, one name always comes to the fore: Henry Edwards Huntington. He came to Southern California in the 1890s and soon became a major "mover and shaker" in its development. The Huntington group incorporated Pacific Electric Railway Company of California on November 12, 1901. The color red was chosen for the PE's livery, so the label "Red Car System" stuck.

Of the total 4,520 PE shares (with a par value of $100 each), Henry E. Huntington owned 986 shares, which was about 22 percent. The other three members of the investment syndicate, Isaias Hellman, Christian DeGuigne, and Antoine Borel, each owned 678 shares. The balance of 1,500 shares went in equal parts to Epes Randolph, John Bicknell, and Jonathan Slauson. Huntington's goal was to build 454 miles of line, and he planned to build to Long Beach and many other points, including a never-built 115-mile line to Santa Barbara. He also set up land companies to acquire large acreages of inexpensive land along the planned interurban routes. The opening of PE's first interurban line, from Los Angeles to Long Beach, coincided with a national holiday, July 4, 1902.

Huntington also got into the power business to tap electricity sources that would be needed as the rail empire grew. With 51 percent ownership by the Huntington group, the Pacific Light and Power Company, a consolidation of many smaller companies, was incorporated on March 6, 1902.

Huntington's ambitious expansion plans dismayed his fellow investors, as he sank profits into more development instead of paying dividends, and one of them, Christian DeGuigne, sold 427 of his shares. Huntington took up 273, and Hellman and Borel each bought 77 shares.

Edward R. Harriman of Southern Pacific (SP) became alarmed that the growing Red Car system would become competition for SP's passenger and freight businesses. So, in 1903, the SP bought up the Hook family's Los Angeles Traction Company, a Huntington rival that included the California Pacific Railway, the interurban line from Los Angeles to San Pedro.

A "battle of the titans" was avoided that year by an agreement between Huntington and Harriman whereby Huntington and SP would be equal owners of PE, purchasing the interests of Hellman, Borel, and DeGuigne's remaining shares, which they would split 50-50. The properties of the former Los Angeles Traction Company (LAT) were transferred to Huntington in exchange for 40.3 percent of the ownership in Pacific Electric, which was equal to Huntington's share.

Huntington transferred the former LAT to the new Los Angeles Inter-Urban Railway (LAIU) and incorporated with himself as the sole owner. Therefore, without SP veto power, his plans for construction of 350 miles of lines continued. Destinations included La Habra and Redlands, as well as Riverside and San Bernardino, Santa Ana, Newport, and the San Fernando Valley. LAIU did not last long due to a national financial downturn. By 1907, it had become the construction arm of PE.

Other acquisitions by PE (Huntington) in the first decade of the 1900s included the Mount Lowe line in 1902, Riverside and Arlington Railway in 1903, Los Angeles and Redondo Railway in 1905, San Bernardino Valley Traction Company in 1907, and Redlands Central Electric Railway Company in 1908. Meanwhile, Harriman took control of another major interurban in the area, the Los Angeles Pacific, which served such areas as Hollywood, Venice, and the Santa Monica Bay communities down to Manhattan Beach, Hermosa Beach, and Redondo Beach.

This book is a summary history of PE, augmented by a gallery of images of various subjects. It concentrates on the Red Cars, so the reader is urged to remember a distinction that *Gillespie's Guide*, one of Los Angeles' many street atlases, summed it up in its revised 1917 edition:

> Two electric railway companies operate in Los Angeles. The Los Angeles Railway system (the yellow cars) practically covers the city, and the Pacific Electric Railway (the red cars), is principally suburban. Los Angeles Railway cars are painted yellow, Pacific Electric Railway cars are painted red.

There is too often confusion about yellow cars and red cars as the memory of them fades with time. Remember that Henry Huntington and associates bought control of LARy in 1898. After his death in 1927, Huntington's estate continued to hold his interest until 1945, when it was sold. Huntington and associates founded PE in 1901 but sold out to Southern Pacific in 1910. It is hoped that this book can help solidify these distinctions and recall an era when people had to time their lives around the PE schedule and thanked their lucky stars for its existence.

One

BEFORE
PACIFIC ELECTRIC

Like many other cities in the United States, Los Angeles began rail-borne transit first with horse cars in 1874, then with cable cars, and then with electrically propelled streetcars running from downtown to residential neighborhoods.

The first interurban, or "between cities," rail service in the Los Angeles area, called the Pasadena and Los Angeles Electric Railway (P&LA), served the two cities in its title and opened in 1895. The two principals in the line, Moses Hazeltine Sherman and his brother-in-law Eli P. Clark, were also building a line toward Santa Monica from Los Angeles called the Pasadena and Pacific Railroad Company (P&P), construction of which began in 1895. The P&LA would be bought by Henry E. Huntington in 1898. The P&LA had become the Los Angeles and Pasadena Electric Railway, while the P&P was replaced by a new entity, Los Angeles–Pacific Railroad, that same year.

Henry Edwards Huntington was the nephew of "Big Four" railroad magnate Collis P. Huntington, president of the Southern Pacific railroad in the 1890s. Henry was his heir apparent for the position.

Henry Huntington came to Southern California in 1898 and soon took control of the existing major streetcar operation, the Los Angeles Railway. He added to it by purchasing other small companies, leaving only Los Angeles Traction Company, owned by the Hook family, and Sherman and Clark's Los Angeles–Pacific as his electric-railway competition. Huntington's long-term goal, however, was a vast interurban rail system for the entire Los Angeles region.

Collis Huntington died suddenly in 1900, but Henry was denied the Southern Pacific presidency. So he sold his large block of SP stock to Edward H. Harriman, who would soon control SP. Huntington turned his energies toward making an interurban system in Southern California a reality while he bought and sold land, which had suddenly appreciated due to the coming of the system.

The first street railway to open in Los Angeles did so in 1874, using—literally—horsepower for propulsion. One or more horses pulled small open-bench cars. By the 1880s, some horse-car lines were converted to cable power, using a wire rope running between the rails, while new lines were built using the newer technology. By the 1890s, both horse and cable power were supplanted by electricity. In this 1889 scene at Temple and Spring Streets in downtown, a northbound horse car, pulled by a team of horses, heads for East Los Angeles. It is passing a southbound train of the Los Angeles Cable Railway, consisting of a dummy, or grip car, and trailer. (Courtesy Metro Library.)

Los Angeles's first interurban railway, the Pasadena and Los Angeles Electric Railway, opened in 1895 and served the Cawston Ostrich Farm in South Pasadena, a tourist hot spot. In 1897, a Chicago syndicate gained control of P&LA and renamed it the Los Angeles and Pasadena Electric Railway. Henry Huntington bought this line in 1898, and it became part of PE in 1902. The tracks of the interurban railway are in the foreground of this 1890s image in front of the ostrich farm. (Courtesy Metro Library.)

Prof. Thaddeus S. C. Lowe built an incredible mountain railway above Pasadena in the early 1890s, known as the Pasadena and Mount Wilson Railway Company. It ran from the Altadena station of the Los Angeles Terminal Railway to Rubio Canyon. This photograph was taken on opening day of the Great Cable Incline, July 4, 1893. It illustrates the counterbalanced cars—"the Rubio" at the bottom of the incline, and the other car, "the Echo," at the top. The incline rose 1,300 vertical feet in 3,000 feet of track with a maximum grade of 62 percent. At the top of Echo Mountain was a hotel and observatory. Also at Echo Mountain was a spectacular narrow-gauge electric line that climbed 3.57 tortuous miles to the summit of Mount Lowe and the $700,000 Ye Alpine Tavern. Professor Lowe had put all of his finances in the mountain railway, and it was put into receivership in 1896; in 1902, the railway was deeded to PE. (Courtesy Metro Library.)

An 1898 view of the top of the Mount Lowe incline shows the second Echo Mountain House, finished in 1894. It burned to the ground in 1900. At right is the observatory, and the buildings in the middle had to do with power generation. A carbarn for the mountain railway to Ye Alpine Tavern was also located here, near the summit, 5,650 feet above sea level. (Courtesy Metro Library.)

Running from Echo Mountain 3.57 miles to Ye Alpine Tavern near the summit of Mount Lowe was this three-foot-six-inch-gauge electric railway, carrying visitors on small open-bench cars. The spectacular route brought forth "oohs" and "ahhs" from riders around each bend. The route had 127 curves and only 225 feet of straight track. (Courtesy Metro Library.)

An 1890s image shows visitors on the verandah of Echo Mountain House looking at the other sites in the complex that became known as "White City." Mother Nature as well as man-made fires, floods, and other disasters bedeviled the Mount Lowe line, bankrupting Professor Lowe and causing the demise of the railway in 1938. (Courtesy Metro Library.)

H. E. HUNTINGTON

Henry Huntington was the subject of many artists at the beginning of the 20th century since he had become a major investor in the Los Angeles area's development. Typical is this drawing from an unknown publication, for Huntington had already become one of the main people involved in the area's growth. (Courtesy Metro Library.)

Two

FOUNDING OF
PACIFIC ELECTRIC

Notable PE accomplishments in the first decade of the 20th century included the building of the giant Pacific shops at Seventh and Alameda Streets and the construction of the nine-story Huntington Building at Sixth and Main Streets in 1905. The latter provided both offices and a downtown terminal for PE.

Construction of the Red Car system continued in the 20th century's first decade and included lines to Long Beach, San Pedro via Wilmington, Santa Ana, Whittier, and Newport Beach. To cite one example of PE's influence, the village of Randolph, which was named in honor of PE chief engineer Epes Randolph, was founded in 1908 in hopes that the honor would accelerate construction of the PE through that location. The name, however, was short lived. In January 1911, Randolph and adjoining Olinda merged to become Brea, which incorporated in 1917 with a population of 752.

Harriman died suddenly in 1909. And at age 60, Huntington's primary interests were increasingly in real estate, electric utilities, and his collections of rare books and art. He prepared to sell his Red Car interests to Southern Pacific but decided to keep the Los Angeles Railway. On November 10, 1910, SP bought out Huntington's 50 percent ownership in PE and sold him in return its ownership in the Los Angeles Railway. The deal was actually much more complex and also included selling to Huntington the portion of the rail lines lying north of about 116th Street for use in the LARy system. As the first decade of the 20th century ended, Henry Huntington had exited the interurban business, but expansion of the Red Car system continued.

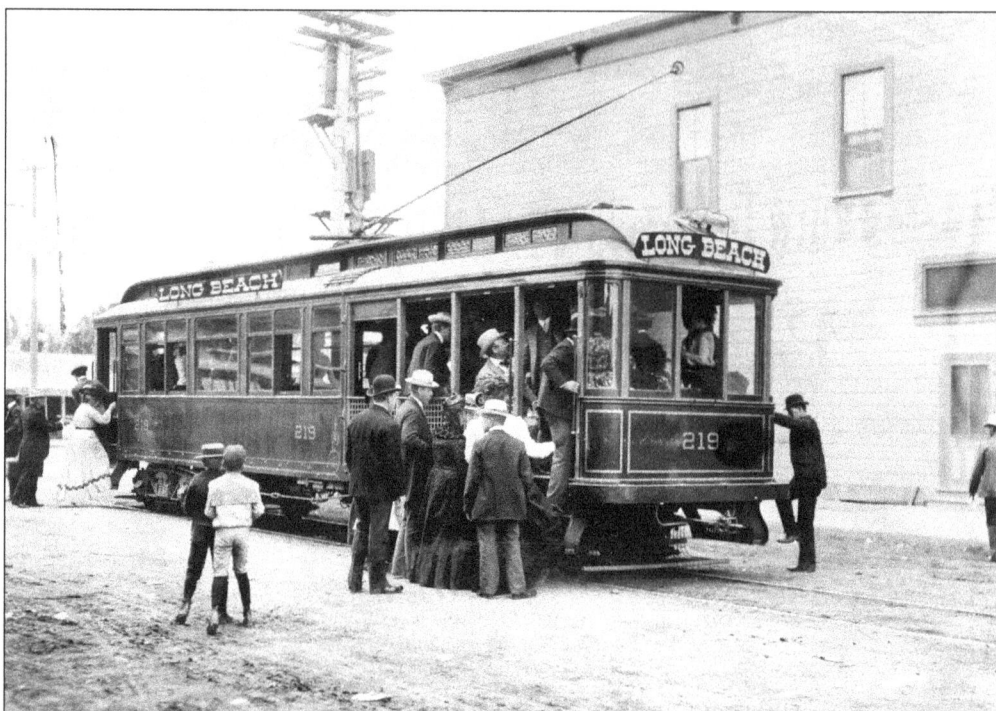

Opening day for the first PE line going from Los Angeles to Long Beach was on July 4, 1902. Here a crowd boards a first-day car. (Courtesy Metro Library.)

Pacific Electric lines served many communities, such as Sierra Madre, whose station is seen in this 1900s photograph. The line opened in 1906. (Courtesy Metro Library.)

A great accomplishment in the first decade of the 20th century was the construction of this massive 10-story structure, at right, which was the largest building west of the Mississippi River for many years. The PE headquarters building and depot at Sixth and Main Streets opened on January 15, 1905. This view, looking north on Main Street, is from 1943. As it was during World War II, ornamental streetlight fixtures were "capped" to prevent their light from shining upward. A deck was added to the building's rear to extend the concourse, which alleviated congestion. (Courtesy Metro Library.)

The Red Car pictured here is about to leave for Los Angeles from the community of Bliss, now North Glendale, in the 1900s. (Courtesy Metro Library.)

Pacific Electric crews gather at Pasadena Car House for a group portrait in the 1900s. Note the white covers slipped over uniform caps and lots of brass to keep polished. (Courtesy Metro Library.)

The first interurban railway, the Pasadena and Los Angeles Electric Railway, built the first line to Pasadena via South Pasadena in 1895. It became part of PE in 1902 and was supplanted by the "Short Line," which Henry Huntington built in 1903. In this 1906 view, this Pasadena-bound car is atop the Daly Street Bridge, which carried it over the Southern Pacific. (Courtesy Metro Library.)

This view looks northeast at the intersection of Main (left to right) and First Streets in the 1900s. A man chats with the traffic policeman, and a Watts Local car awaits permission to turn south onto Main Street. (Courtesy Metro Library.)

Oneonta Park, named for Henry Huntington's birthplace in New York State, was an important junction on PE, where Short Line cars from Pasadena joined a four-track at Fair Oaks Avenue and Huntington Drive, which also served Pasadena via the Oak Knoll, Sierra Madre, and Monrovia–Glendora lines. This early 20th-century rural scene contrasts with this area's suburban development in intervening decades. (Courtesy Metro Library.)

When building the electric railway line to Glendale and Burbank, PE constructed this magnificent pile trestle to span a gap in the hills in 1904. Its trestle was modified in 1928 with the substitution of steel girders in its middle, allowing clearance for building Fletcher Drive underneath it. This view, from the Riverside Drive side, was taken in 1914. (Courtesy Craig Rasmussen Collection.)

The opening of the first PE line, the route from Los Angeles to Long Beach, was a marketing success. It became one of the heaviest traveled Red Car lines. This early 1900s view shows the giant pavilion that shaded those who liked to experience ocean breezes out of the sun and an early Pine Avenue pier. Both are now gone. (Courtesy Metro Library.)

Watts was where the Southern District's four-track line became a two-track line, with routes to Santa Ana, Redondo Beach, and other South Bay communities. This 1906 image looks southeast. The Long Beach line continued south with the Newport–Balboa and San Pedro lines branching off at other junctions. The semaphore signals, controlled by Watts Tower, were labeled "San Pedro," "Newport," "Santa Ana," and "Long Beach" on their blades. (Courtesy Metro Library.)

This two-car train of Red Cars destined for San Pedro is about to cross 103rd Street around 1906. The view is northward, in contrast to the other photograph on the proceeding page. (Courtesy Metro Library.)

Three

THE GREAT MERGER, OPENING OF THE LONGEST LINE

1911–1920

By the second decade of the 20th century, Southern Pacific controlled the Pacific Electric and other rail companies that Henry Huntington had originally bought as well as the Los Angeles–Pacific. So SP decided to consolidate all the entities, and on August 24, 1911, a "new" Pacific Electric Railway was incorporated. It began operations on September 1.

This was known as "the Great Merger," bringing together eight entities: Pacific Electric Railway Company, Los Angeles Inter-Urban Railway Company, Los Angeles and Redondo Railway Company, The Riverside and Arlington Railway Company, The San Bernardino Valley Traction Company, Redlands Central Railway Company, San Bernardino Inter-Urban Railway Company, and Los Angeles Pacific Company. The one remaining independent in the Inland Empire, the Ontario and San Antonio Heights Railroad Company, sold out to PE. This is why Huntington's operation became known as the "old" PE. This left only one independent interurban in the Los Angeles area, the Glendale and Montrose Railway.

A notable accomplishment of the second decade of the 20th century was completion of the nearly 58-mile San Bernardino line, which meant closing a 20-mile gap between Upland and San Bernardino. Now the lines in the Inland Empire were linked to the rest of the system, albeit the "San Berdoo" line ran on a higher voltage than the local lines. Another major capital improvement to the Red Car system was the building of the 125-acre Torrance shops in 1916–1917. The second decade of the 20th century was the zenith of PE. At that time, it had over 1,000 miles of track and served 125 communities in Los Angeles, Orange, Riverside, and San Bernardino Counties. Plans for lines beyond in the more rural outer counties did not become a reality. However, the Red Car system provided passenger and freight service, facilitating much growth in the four counties.

PE's first foray into motor buses came in 1917, when local streetcar service from San Bernardino to nearby Highland and Patton was supplemented by buses. It would be four years until the next bus line began. It was clear that PE was first and foremost a rail operation, with buses only used for connecting or shuttle lines.

Unregulated jitney buses often were just automobiles, and they shuttled passengers as early as 1914. In the jargon of the time, a "jit" was a nickel. The jitneys paralleled streetcar and interurban rail lines, skimming off some of the traffic with cheaper fares. But most of these often undependable enterprises soon disappeared or were legislated out of existence. Because most people still depended on the streetcars and interurban trains, America's entry into World War I did not have a significant effect on the Red Car system.

In the days before the family automobile was commonplace, residents and tourists alike would see sights on special-excursion cars on PE. This 1914 view shows PE crewmen on break during "the Old Mission Tour" at Mission San Gabriel. (Courtesy Craig Rasmussen Collection.)

Additional lines and patronage created the need to augment terminal facilities at Sixth and Main Streets. Surface tracks entering from Seventh Street are shown at center right. The elevated depot and ramp down to San Pedro Street were opened in 1916. This view of the $250,000 facility dates from about that year. (Courtesy Metro Library.)

To serve patrons of Southern Pacific long-distance trains, PE began service from the Pasadena SP depot to Shorb in Alhambra in 1912. This service continued until 1933. (Courtesy Craig Rasmussen Collection.)

Typical of PE cars used in local service in the early part of the 20th century was No. 227, seen about 1919 on Glendale Boulevard in Los Angeles. It was built by the St. Louis Car Company about 1909 for the "old" Huntington-era Pacific Electric. It was scrapped in 1927. (Courtesy Metro Library.)

PE's early foray into buses occurred about 1916–1917, when parent Southern Pacific ordered four of these tractor-trailer articulated vehicles, one of which was used in the San Bernardino/Redlands area by PE. (Courtesy Metro Library.)

This 1920s view of downtown Glendale, looking south from Broadway, shows a PE car southbound to downtown Los Angeles. It also shows something ominous, a hoard of automobiles, which would win out over Pacific Electric as first choice for transport. By 1919, Los Angeles County had nearly 141,000 gas buggies. (Courtesy Metro Library.)

Pacific Electric's longest route already served Covina, as seen here in 1912. Two years later, San Bernardino was reached, and using the Inland Empire routes that were included in the 1911 merger, many other communities in that easternmost region, such as Riverside and Redlands, were added to the list of destinations. (Courtesy Metro Library.)

The motorman and conductors of this six-car Venice Short Line train are ready to load up for a trip from its Santa Monica terminal to Hill Street station in downtown Los Angeles in 1916. Unlike some PE Western District lines, this line continued to use the surface terminal at Hill Street until it was converted to bus operation in 1950. (Courtesy Craig Rasmussen Collection.)

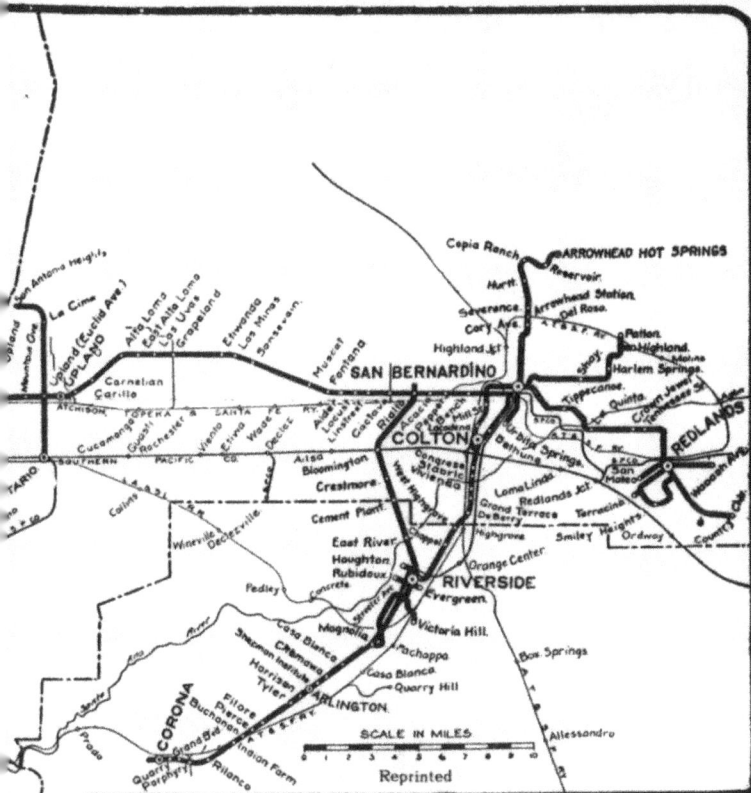

This system map of Pacific Electric dates from the early 1920s, when the system was at its peak, using 1,164 miles of track, 2,700 trains a day, and 950 passenger cars. (Courtesy Metro Library.)

SCALE IN MILES

Reprinted

MOUNT LOWE
MILE HIGH SCENIC TOUR THROUGH WONDERLAND $2⁵⁰

Not Equalled by any Trolley Trip in the World at any Price

5 TRAINS DAILY: 8, 9, 10 A. M.; 1:30, 4 P.M., FROM **MAIN ST. STATION**

MOUNT LOWE RESORT, HIGH UP ON THE FAMOUS MOUNTAIN, PROVIDES EVERY COMFORT.

ORANGE EMPIRE TROLLEY TRIP
To RIVERSIDE REDLANDS SAN BERNARDINO $4⁰⁰

Visiting Famous Mission Inn at Riverside and Smiley Heights at Redlands

A DAY'S JOURNEY OF 175 MILES THROUGH THE CITRUS BELT AND ITS CITIES

Guide-Lecturer; Special Car   9 A.M. Daily from Main St. Station

"Old Mission—Balloon Route" TROLLEY TRIP

TWO DOLLARS' WORTH OF PLEASURE $1⁵⁰
TWO DAYS' TRAVEL REDUCED TO ONE, FOR

MANY FREE ATTRACTIONS ENROUTE
AND NOVEL SIGHTS EACH MILE AND EACH TURN OF THE ROAD

THREE DAYS OF PROGRAMMED PLEASURE FOR THE TOURIST, UNEXCELLED ANYWHERE

BEAUTIFUL ILLUSTRATED FOLDERS GIVE ALL DETAILS
ASK FOR ONE AT INFORMATION BUREAUS.

A bathing beauty poses with her trophy for some sort of contest at the Redondo Beach shore in the early 1900s. PE served a large building that provided a plunge (swimming pool) and restaurant. Both the facility and the beach were magnets for area travelers in those days. (Courtesy Metro Library.)

This front-page artwork adorned a picture folder that contained a souvenir image taken at the top of the Mount Lowe incline (Echo Mountain). Such images resided in many Southern California homes and other locations to recall the thrill of a day trip to Mount Lowe. (Courtesy Metro Library.)

Four

THE AUTOMOBILE AGE BEGINS
1921–1930

The halcyon days of the Red Car system came to an end in the 1920s and 1930s. The biggest negative for the system was the development of automobiles and roads, which caused many people to switch to private transportation. Additional roads brought an outcry for more grade crossings, which slowed down the railcars and increased hazards. The mileage of roads and the number of automobiles took a big leap, all at a heavy cost to the PE. The opening of a one-mile subway in 1925 eliminated slow, downtown street trackage for a few lines. Still basically a rail system with some buses, the PE began a steady downhill slide to bus operation.

A rival franchise scheme led PE and Los Angeles Railway to create a joint bus operation, the Los Angeles Motor Bus Company, in 1923. The name later changed to the Los Angeles Motor Coach Company. Besides the major problem outlined above, an electricity shortage about 1924 caused many marginal rail lines to either be eliminated or converted to buses. However, the company still felt it was a rail system, with buses serving a minor role. Things rolled along until October 1929, when the stock market crashed. The resulting Great Depression brought financial ruin to companies and individuals. PE was no exception, and it took harsh measures to simply survive, though the handwriting was on the wall that tough times would continue.

The operator of a PE bus on the East Washington line in Pasadena takes a break at the Tierra Alta end of the line. Many of PE's local lines were converted to bus operations in the 1920s. (Courtesy Metro Library.)

One of the most notable events in PE's history was the November 30, 1925, opening of a one-mile subway from Fourth and Hill Streets to Glendale and Beverly Boulevards. It included a new substation, No. 51 Toluca, and a new five-track station known as the "Subway Terminal" in the basement of a new office building (with a new height limit of 150 feet) on the west side of Hill Street between Fourth and Fifth Streets. This view of opening ceremonies is at the outer end of the bore, where Toluca Yard was located. (Courtesy Metro Library.)

Ceremonies for the opening of the Subway Terminal brought forth a mass doffing of hats during that November day. (Courtesy Metro Library)

A southbound Vineyard local car (Vineyard was on the Venice Short Line) is on Hill Street at Second Street in downtown Los Angeles in February 1948 (note the southern side of the Hill Streets behind). Also note the ornate standard streetlight that partially obscures the Acme semaphore traffic signal. (Courtesy Craig Rasmussen Collection.)

Pictured here in 1927 is a line of Pasadena PE buses. (Courtesy Metro Library.)

Car 146, seen here in front of the Pasadena Car House on Fair Oaks in 1914, was built in 1907 for the San Bernardino Valley Traction Company, one of the Inland Empire operations folded into the "new" PE in the 1911 merger. The car was sent to scrap in 1927. (Courtesy Metro Library.)

Looking north in 1924 on Hill Street, at Ninth Street, an example of dual-gauge track is seen. The PE Cars, which were red, used the two outer rails, and were laid four feet, eight and a half inches apart. Los Angeles Railway cars, which were yellow, used the two inner rails, which were three-foot-six-inch gauge. (Courtesy Metro Library.)

In 1922, PE received the first 50 of its 600–759 Series "Hollywood" cars. Altogether there would be 160 of the steel cars. Their introduction into service allowed retirement of the last of PE's wood cars on local routes. (Courtesy Metro Library.)

In this 1928 photograph, a limited train from Long Beach to Los Angeles is poised to leave the oceanside city as soon as the uniformed crew and a few other men finish posing for the camera. (Courtesy Craig Rasmussen Collection.)

A group of car men and a clerk pose in 1925 with the jovial passenger service director (left) at the elevated rail station behind the big PE building at Sixth and Main Streets. The man with the stars on his sleeve must have lots of "whiskers," parlance for seniority. (Courtesy Metro Library.)

Steel interurban Car No. 1209, seen at the PE surface yard at Sixth and Main Streets depot, epitomizes the best of the Red Cars (the 1200 Series). (Courtesy Metro Library.)

This 1922 photograph looks west down Hollywood Boulevard from Wilcox Street. A Red Car would soon arrive from Los Angeles. (Courtesy Metro Library.)

A contractor's crew chews away at a hill during construction of the Subway Terminal building on the west side of Hill Street on the block between Fourth and Fifth Streets. In 1924, the 10-story office structure was at the height limit—150 feet—for that time. The giant building continued the 1920s trend away from residential occupancy and toward commercial use in the neighborhood. (Courtesy Metro Library.)

Erection of the steel skeleton of the $4 million Subway Terminal building, which contained the five-track PE terminal in its basement, was completed in 1925. The building opened in 1926. The Subway Terminal Corporation, composed of many big names in Los Angeles, was formed to construct the office building. (Courtesy Metro Library.)

Five

THE GREAT DEPRESSION
AND MORE BUSES
1931–1940

In the 1930s, the Pacific Electric and other rail empires started to shrink. The cheaper transportation mode of buses required the presence of only one employee on board, the driver. Buses also became the preferred way to avoid the expense of maintaining the physical plant for upkeep on railcars.

Had not the rumblings of war begun in Europe with the rise of Nazi Germany and the forming of the Axis powers, the PE would have abandoned much of its aging rail system, either abolishing service or converting to bus operation. But with apprehension about the future involvement of the United States in a seemingly inevitable global conflict, the PE maintained its status quo.

In 1939, the opening of the first superhighway in the area, the Arroyo Seco Parkway, forecast what would be a continuing trend in coming years: dependency on the private automobile as the area's principal means of passenger transportation.

In this photograph, the January 1, 1937, Rose Parade had recently ended, and some of the sidewalk audience had boarded a train of PE 950s for a return trip to downtown Los Angeles. (Courtesy E. M. Leo/Craig Rasmussen Collection.)

A great advance in traffic circulation, as well as the elimination of a hazardous grade crossing, was marked by the February 20, 1937, opening of a viaduct over Huntington Drive at Soto Street, where it turned into Mission Road. This photograph shows the progress of construction in April 1936. After abandonment of that last PE operation in its Northern District in 1951, the former track right-of-way was made into a roadway, taking Soto Street over the intersection. (Courtesy Ivan Baker/Craig Rasmussen Collection.)

A portion of PE's line to the San Fernando Valley opened in 1912, and was considerably upgraded in the Cahuenga Pass in 1940, when the first PE car ran on new track, relocating the rail line to the new Hollywood Freeway's median. In the background is the Mulholland Drive Bridge. The first segment west from Highland Avenue to the bridge was completed on January 15, 1940. The second segment of the freeway, from Mulholland to near the Barham Boulevard overpass, opened November 30, 1940. The third segment (the PE tracks parted here) to Vineland Avenue opened in 1948. Rail service on the PE line quit December 28, 1952. The empty right-of-way became one additional lane each way for the 101 Freeway in 1965. (Courtesy Craig Rasmussen Collection.)

The big Red Cars served many Southern California communities, such as Pomona. In this September 29, 1940, view, No. 1220 in seen on Garey Avenue at the Union Pacific and Southern Pacific grade crossing. This portion of the PE was a casualty of rail-to-bus conversions in 1941. (Courtesy Frank Bradford/Craig Rasmussen Collection.)

Buses were replacing railcars in the 1930s. A freshly delivered 31-seat bus, built by the Twin Coach Company, gets its official portrait made in front of the brick office building at PE's giant Torrance shops in 1940. (Courtesy Metro Library.)

In 1929, PE rebuilt a 3,160-foot portion of its Northern District in the community of El Sereno, near South Pasadena, with deluxe overhead wire carried on these latticework poles. The poles were acquired secondhand from the Visalia Electric Railroad in California's Great Central Valley. Some historians refer to this as PE's "dream" trackage. (Courtesy Craig Rasmussen Collection.)

Speaking of deluxe, a portion on PE's San Fernando Valley line through Cahuenga Pass was upgraded so the tracks ran in the median of the Hollywood Freeway. This March 10, 1940, view shows a PE car under the Pilgrimage Play Bridge, looking toward the valley. The bridge is still there, and the Pilgrimage Play Bowl is now called the John Anson Ford Amphitheatre, named after a late Los Angeles County supervisor. (Courtesy Craig Rasmussen Collection.)

The massive Seventh Street Surface Yard of the Sixth and Main Streets depot was a forerunner of the elevated station, which opened in 1916. A temporary surface terminal with train sheds was built so that all cars would not have to go through the headquarters building's concourse onto Main Street, where a terrible backup had developed. When the elevated station opened, more and more PE cars went up the ramp from San Pedro Street. By the 1930s, the surface yard was used for daytime storage or for box motors. The space occupied by the Red Cars in this 1941 view of its northwest corner was used to build a two-story bus station (on the lower level) with provision for bus parking on the roof in 1942. Obviously the transportation trend was moving toward buses. (Courtesy Craig Rasmussen Collection.)

The Redondo Beach via Del Rey line reached the shore at Del Rey and ran through Manhattan and Hermosa Beaches to its Redondo Beach terminal. It was part of the Los Angeles Pacific system, which was added to the PE in the 1911 merger. This view is just below Del Rey, a community now known as Playa Del Rey, and was taken in November 1939. The line was abandoned in May 1940. (Courtesy Craig Rasmussen Collection.).

The crossing of Aliso Street over the Los Angeles River, just east of downtown, occurred on this rickety 1903 vintage bridge. The structure was at street level, had hazardous railroad grade crossings at both ends, and provided only a single lane in each direction for automotive traffic. This bridge was closed and demolished in 1940, when PE traffic detoured to the Macy (now Chavez) Street crossing. A new replacement span, built at a cost of $3,605,000, opened in 1943. The new bridge was part of the Ramona (now San Bernardino) and Santa Ana Parkway plan. PE's share of the cost was $231,000. Due to automobiles shifting to the new Aliso route, traffic was as bad as ever. (Courtesy Metro Library.)

Leaving the line to Redondo Beach, at Hermosillo (near Gardena), Car No. 818 headed south to San Pedro. This was known as the San Pedro via Torrance line, built as the narrow-gauge California Pacific. This view was taken on New Year's Day 1939. Note the station design, an architectural style used on many PE wayside stops. (Courtesy W.C. Whittaker/Jim Walker Collection.)

Built in 1918, the Bellflower PE station was on the east side of Bellflower Boulevard. Rail passenger service was cut back to this point in 1950, and the entire route was converted to bus operation in 1958. As built, the passenger waiting area was open, as seen in this 1930s view. In later years, it was enclosed. The building still exists and is one of the few visible reminders of the Red Cars. (Courtesy Metro Library.)

This photograph shows Car No. 892 after it had just arrived at the Burbank Station in November 1939. The station was on the south side of Glenoaks Boulevard and Palm Avenue, and it was replaced by a smaller, flat-roof structure in 1949. (Courtesy Craig Rasmussen Collection.)

From the downtown Long Beach terminal at Pacific Avenue and Ocean Boulevard, the East Seventh local line went north on Pacific Avenue, then east on First Street, north on Pine Avenue, and east on Seventh Street to Redondo Avenue. All remaining Long Beach local rail lines quit in 1940, and a local bus operator took over. In July 1939, Birney Safety Car No. 385 heads east on Seventh Street at Cherry Avenue. (Courtesy Craig Rasmussen Collection.)

At the foot of the viaduct from the Sixth and Main Streets depot, a steel Red Car en route to Long Beach turns south onto San Pedro Street in 1940. (Courtesy Craig Rasmussen Collection.)

At its single-track terminal on Vine Street on the north side of Hollywood Boulevard, a Hollywood-type car on the Western–Franklin route would soon ritually change ends and head for the other end of the line at Western Avenue and Santa Monica Boulevard, the location of the terminal in later years. (Courtesy Craig Rasmussen Collection.)

One of the branches of the San Bernardino route turned off at Rialto and ran south to Riverside. No. 1209 is at Bloomington Tower at the crossing of the Southern Pacific. This view was taken on June 8, 1940, the last day of passenger service. (Courtesy Harold F. Stewart/Craig Rasmussen Collection.)

Among the rail services of the PE in and around the San Bernardino area, the longest lasting was the line to Colton. A car is seen southbound on E Street next to the PE depot. It served passengers for Southern Pacific trains. Passenger service stopped on February 22, 1942, and the line was totally abandoned a month later, on April 23. (Courtesy Craig Rasmussen Collection.)

One of PE's local rail lines in Pasadena ran up Fair Oaks Avenue to Altadena, where a single-truck Birney Safety Car is seen at Montana Avenue, near the border between the two communities. In a photograph, taken on January 17, 1941, Lawrence Hunt, who performed the duties of both motorman and conductor on the little streetcar, poses in front of it. (Courtesy Craig Rasmussen Collection.)

In downtown Alhambra, wooden PE interurban Car No. 1024 moves westbound on Main Street near Sixth Street in 1941. The Alhambra–San Gabriel–Temple City route was converted to a bus operation on November 29, 1941, just a few days before the Pearl Harbor attack and the United States' entry into World War II. (Courtesy Craig Rasmussen Collection.)

Four PE tracks of the Southern District main were built on this bridge over the busy Firestone Boulevard in the south Los Angeles community of Graham in June 1937. Temporary at-grade tracks were used for rail traffic during construction. A policeman stops motor vehicle traffic while a PE rail crane places girders on the $300,000 structure. All went well until the 1980s, when it was decided during the selection of specifications for the Metro Blue Line that the bridge had to be replaced due to clearance problems. Then the replacement bridge collapsed during construction, and a replacement for it had to be assembled from scratch. (Courtesy Metro Library.)

Two cars from the 1200 Series heads for the ocean as a Long Beach Limited train in the 1940s atop the Firestone Boulevard Bridge. (Courtesy Metro Library.)

PE Car No. 842 rests between trips in July 1937 at Canoga Park at the west end of the San Fernando Valley. The 800 Series (800–929) were built for the "old" PE in batches from 1902 to 1906. Most of these wooden interurbans were scrapped before World War II. (Courtesy Craig Rasmussen Collection.)

This photograph shows outbound Car No. 745 (in "Valley Seven" livery) stopped on December 14, 1938, at Kester Junction, just west of North Hollywood station, the end of a block of joint PE–Southern Pacific operations. At this point, SP would veer diagonally northwest. The SP Burbank branch is the alignment for today's Orange Line bus rapid-transit line, which opened in 2005. (Courtesy Craig Rasmussen Collection.)

A two-car train heads east on Colorado Boulevard in downtown Pasadena at Madison Avenue about 1947. Posters for the 1948 Rose Parade with the theme of "childhood memories" hang from the PE's span wires. The train turned south at Lake Avenue, on the Oak Knoll route for its trip back to Los Angeles. (Courtesy Metro Library.)

Red Car No. 843 pauses at the Sierra Vista station, just west of Alhambra, in the late 1930s. It would soon be on its way to its Watts terminal, at 103rd Street. (Courtesy Metro Library.)

This backward-forward looking bus was built for PE by Fageol in 1931. Called a "Metropolitan," it had 28 seats. The front is at right, and the doors were only on the curbside. (Courtesy Metro Library.)

Six

WARTIME AND POSTWAR DEVELOPMENTS
1941–1950

The calendar year of 1940 saw a gearing up for what seemed to be an inevitable war. With the entry of the nation into what would be World War II after the December 7, 1941, attack by the Japanese on the U.S. naval fleet at Pearl Harbor, the Pacific Electric's resources would be stretched "for the duration."

New buses were generally vetoed, so railcars that had reached the end of their economic life soldiered on to carry the horde of more riders. Unexpected rail business was created by gasoline rationing. Many people required transportation to wartime industries. PE's freight operations were also put to increased use to move defense materials throughout the Los Angeles region. PE had not had a profitable year since 1925, but during the war and the early postwar years of 1942–1946, the Red Car system showed a plus in the income column.

However, the freeway frenzy resumed by 1947, and PE patrons became automobile owners as ridership severely declined on all modes of public transportation. Seeing no end to money-losing rail passenger operations, PE chose massive conversion to buses. The joint PE-LATL Los Angeles Motor Coach operation was dissolved in 1949, with each owner taking some of the routes and buses.

A freight train chugs along at La Verne in 1944. The steam locomotive, leased by PE from parent Southern Pacific, is assisted by two "juice jack" electric locomotives, which not only boosted horsepower but also used their trolley poles to actuate grade-crossing signals, which used the overhead wire as a circuit. The two electric units were built in PE's own Torrance shops. (Courtesy Craig Rasmussen Collection.)

PE's assistance to the World War II home front effort included moving troops, like these members of the Army Air Corps. (Courtesy Metro Library.)

Members of the military board a PE train at the elevated rail depot at Sixth and Main Streets during World War II. (Courtesy Craig Rasmussen Collection.)

Wartime gas rationing brought an upsurge in ridership on PE lines. Wooden cars that were ready to be retired, such as this train of Ten Hundreds at Watts-103rd in 1943, soldiered on during the conflict. They were not sent to scrap until 1950. (Courtesy Craig Rasmussen Collection.)

Construction of the California Shipbuilding Corporation (Calship) facility on Terminal Island during the war by the U.S. Maritime Commission to build troop and materiel transports included a Calship Railway. It ran off the island and used PE rails to transport many workers who, due to gas rationing, could not use their own automobiles. Cars were brought from recently abandoned suburban-electric railways in the San Francisco Bay Area, such as this five-car train headed for Calship just south of Amoco Junction in 1944. The wisps of smoke are from a passing steam locomotive. (Courtesy Craig Rasmussen Collection.)

A PE Presidents' Conference Car (PCC) streamliner of the North Glendale branch of the Glendale–Burbank line has just arrived at the Mountain Avenue terminal on Brand Boulevard in the 1940s. The "presidents" referred to the heads of electric railways, as most city-transit systems at that time still used streetcars. (Courtesy Metro Library.)

A 100-class city streetcar is en route to its home on PE's Western District Echo Park Avenue in 1947. It heads west on Sixth Street, at the corner of Main Street in downtown. Later that year, Sixth Street became an eastbound one-way street, which paired with the westbound one-way thoroughfare of Fifth Street. (Courtesy Metro Library.)

Headed west on Fourth Street in Santa Ana, this two-car train of "Twelve Hundred" is about to leave the street track at Artesia Street and enter a private right-of-way while inbound to Los Angeles in July 1946. (Courtesy Metro Library.)

Some time in the 1940s, the last full decade for the remainder the Northern District rail lines, a Los Angeles–bound PE car passes through Indian Village, the south end of the "four-tracks of the North." This was near its meeting with other lines at Valley Junction (near today's L.A. State College station of Metrolink). (Courtesy Metro Library.)

Trains of Red Cars in the late 1940s are at a halt on Fair Oaks Avenue in Pasadena as they await in queue the conclusion of the annual Rose Parade along Colorado Boulevard. (Courtesy Metro Library.)

A special three-car train of "Hollywood" cars heads east on Sixth Street at Broadway in downtown Los Angeles on a New Year's Day during the 1940s, headed for Rose Parade in Pasadena. The Sixth Street trackage was a link to PE's Western District. (Courtesy Craig Rasmussen Collection.)

PE "Hollywood" Car No. 605, en route to Sierra Vista from Watts, heads north on Main Street at Fifth Street in 1949. (Courtesy Craig Rasmussen Collection.)

As part of the 1947 modifications on the Sixth and Main Streets depot, the bridge across Los Angeles Street (view looks north) was replaced by a wider span. The bus at the curb hauled construction workers. (Courtesy Metro Library.)

Passengers board buses in this 1940s eastward view of the concourse at the Sixth and Main Streets depot. (Courtesy Metro Library.)

This 1944 view of the west end of the Beverly Hills PE station, at Santa Monica Boulevard and Canon Drive, shows Red Cars and Red Buses. Car No. 740 is at the end of the Beverly Hills–via–Hollywood Boulevard route (note the wartime hood over its headlight). Bus No. 2513 is going to Santa Monica via Brentwood, and Bus No. 2521 is on the Hollywood–to–Santa Monica–via–Vineyard route. The track in the foreground is part of the Sherman Cutoff. (Courtesy Metro Library.)

A Newport Beach–bound car passes through sandy Los Patos in the 1940s. Tower Car No. 00160 sits on a siding. This oceanside location's name meant "the ducks" and was home to the Pacific Electric Rod and Gun Club, an employee-recreation group. (Courtesy Harold F. Stewart/Craig Rasmussen Collection.)

The controls for one of these cars, nicknamed "blimps" for their large size, brought down from the San Francisco Bay Area during World War II, are shown in this cab view. At left is the controller, at center is the brake stand, and at right is the whistle valve and cord. Meters (out of sight, above) indicated air pressure. (Courtesy Metro Library.)

Pictured here in their last years of service, the 1000 Series, or Ten Hundreds, await their next assignment at Macy Street yard northeast of downtown Los Angeles. (Courtesy Metro Library.)

64

In the final years for the Red Cars, these owl-faced blimp cars made up the bulk of PE's rail car fleet. Here Car No. 450, which once ran on Southern Pacific's suburban network in the San Francisco East Bay Area, is at Macy Street Yard in Los Angeles in the late 1940s. (Courtesy Metro Library.)

One of the cars brought down from the Bay Area during World War II to augment the PE fleet crosses Main Street Seal Beach en route to Newport Beach in 1946. (Courtesy Craig Rasmussen Collection.)

Heading north on Highland Avenue for the San Fernando Valley, PE No. 736 stops to take a crowd of passengers at Hollywood Boulevard in 1948. Now a retail-and-entertainment center sits at this famous intersection. (Courtesy Metro Library.)

This Red Car, the first to go east down the viaduct to San Pedro, then north and east to Pasadena, leaves the Sixth and Main Streets elevated depot at 5:58 a.m. on October 5, 1947. Sixth Street had just become an eastbound one-way street. Its westbound mate was Fifth Street. (Courtesy Metro Library.)

A Newport Beach car heads toward the resort community on the shoreline electric route near Huntington Beach on June 12, 1947. (Courtesy Craig Rasmussen Collection.)

Two rail tunnels along Hill Street in downtown Los Angeles were bored in 1910 to form a link between downtown and Sunset Boulevard. A motor-vehicle bore was added to the south tunnel (between First and Temple Streets) in 1919, but there wasn't one added to the second tunnel, which swung west to almost a diagonal northwest route for its trip to Sunset Boulevard from Temple Street. This 1942 view from First Street shows a downtown-bound Echo Park Avenue car. The last use of these tunnels for PE rail service was October 1, 1950. Construction of the Hollywood Freeway in the 1950s obliterated much of the hills through which both tunnels ran. (Courtesy Craig Rasmussen Collection.)

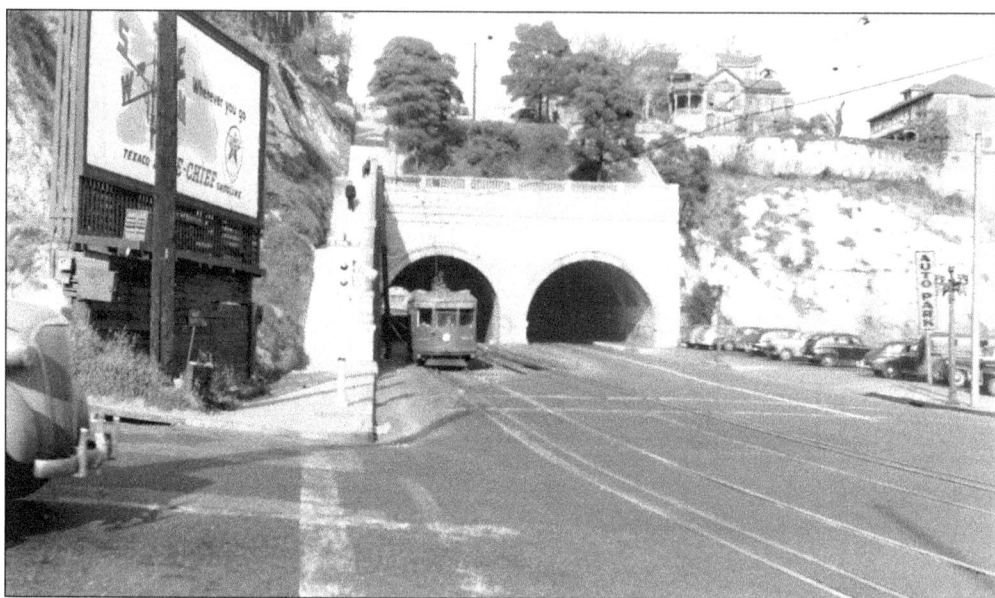

The southernmost Hill Street tunnel, between First and Temple Streets, was also used by the Los Angeles Railway's (Los Angeles Transit Lines after January 10, 1945) narrow-gauge, three-foot-six-inch trackage (note the third rail). The A and L streetcar lines began using the tunnel July 6, 1939. While the L line changed downtown terminals (to Spring Street and Sunset Boulevard) on September 24 of that year, the A line continued to use it until it was converted to buses on June 30, 1946. This is an Echo Park Avenue car headed south on Hill Street to downtown stores. (Courtesy Craig Rasmussen Collection.)

The north side of the southern Hill Street tunnel at Temple Street shows the portals of the two bores (the 1919 motor-vehicle addition is at left). This 1949 view was taken after much of the Los Angeles Transit Lines trackage, which curved here, was gone. The car heads for a turnback at Gardner Junction, west of downtown Hollywood at Sunset Boulevard. (Courtesy Jim Walker Collection.)

This 1949 view, looking out the north rail portal of the Hill Street Tunnel, shows a vestige of the dual-gauge track that was used for a few years in the southern tunnel. (Courtesy Jim Walker Collection.)

One of the 100-class PE cars, purchased new in 1930, heads north out of the north Hill Street Tunnel in the last few days of its use in June 1950. Soon PE Car No. 104 will be westbound in the middle of Sunset Boulevard, turning on Echo Park Avenue in the community of the same name. (Courtesy Craig Rasmussen Collection.)

During the 1950 horseracing season at Santa Anita Racetrack, which began the same day as the Rose Bowl football game in Pasadena, a three-car train of "Hollywood" cars brings a full load of horseracing fans to the track. After the last rail service in 1951, buses took over. The Santa Anita spur came off the Monrovia–Glendora line just west of Arcadia. (Courtesy Metro Library.)

Until the end of the 1940s, PE crews would wear brass buttons and identification insignias with the name of the company and their position (motorman, conductor, etc. on hats and lapels). A crew poses in front of a blimp interurban car in the 1940s. Soon after, they were issued bus driver–style hat badges. (Courtesy Metro Library.)

The motorman (in overalls) and one of the conductors pose in front of this three-car train of Red Cars on the inbound track of the Monrovia–Glendora line between Duarte and East Duarte. (Courtesy Craig Rasmussen Collection.)

Passenger Agent H. O. Marler (left) poses with PE president O. A. Smith (second from right) and two unidentified naval officers at the Sixth and Main Streets depot's elevated-train platform in 1942 during the ceremonial "unveiling" of a specially painted streamliner promoting enlistment in the armed forces for World War II. (Courtesy Metro Library.)

Sometime during World War II, a five-car special Calship heads for Terminal Island and is just about to cross Ninety-second Street. Graham Yard is seen at left. (Courtesy Metro Library.)

Many Calship employees are among the throng heading for the shipyard special train at the Sixth and Main Streets depot during World War II. (Courtesy Metro Library.)

PE trains and buses brought many military personnel to San Bernardino during World War II. (Courtesy Metro Library.)

This photograph, taken at the end of World War II, September 15, 1945, looks east on Sixth Street at the Pacific Electric Building. The intersection was festooned with paper as the office staff joins into the celebration of VJ Day. (Courtesy Metro Library.)

In 1948, the annual Los Angeles County Fair was at the county fairgrounds in Pomona and was served by PE cars and buses. A three-car train unloads passengers at the special platform. The first fair at Pomona opened October 17, 1922, and ran for five days. Red Car trains served the fair from 1946 to 1950. (Courtesy Metro Library.)

A two-car train of steel PE interurbans heads for Long Beach in Willowbrook in the late 1940s. (Courtesy Metro Library.)

One of PE's Red Cars gets ready to leave for Los Angeles. In this 1943 image, the car sits at the Newport Beach station. The bus facing away from the camera will carry passengers to Balboa. (Courtesy Craig Rasmussen Collection.)

In this 1940s view, looking north, one of the 30 PCC streamliners in PE's 5000 Series sits south of the West Hollywood shops (the brick building at rear). (Courtesy Metro Library.)

A PE bus built by White Motors of Cleveland, Ohio, is about to go through the washer in this photograph, looking northeast, at Macy Street Yard in the 1940s. White produced, among other products, trucks and sewing machines. The firm was founded in 1876 and closed in 1980. (Courtesy Metro Library.)

This appears to be an official publicity shot of a PE Red Car alongside a red bus built by White Motors. The two vehicles are in the Seventh Street Surface Yard in the 1940s. Behind them at left is the two-story Los Angeles Street bus station with roof parking. (Courtesy Metro Library.)

The PE steel interurban car pictured here originally was built for a system out of Portland, Oregon. The nickname "Portland Twelves" was given to the cars of this series that came to Southern California in 1928. This view, looking northwest at Bellflower station, was taken in 1941 shortly before the second track of a large portion of the Santa Ana line was removed. (Courtesy Craig Rasmussen.)

In this 1946 photograph, a two-car train of "Hollywood" cars has just crossed Lankershim Boulevard in North Hollywood and will soon go west to Kester Junction (Ethel Avenue), where the SP will turn diagonally north (site of today's Orange Line) and continue on to Van Nuys. The wooden station, in shadow at right, served both PE and parent Southern Pacific trains. (Courtesy Craig Rasmussen Collection.)

In downtown Pasadena in the 1940s, a westbound PE car signed for the Short Line is westbound on Colorado Boulevard at Fair Oaks Avenue, where it will turn left and go through South Pasadena, then turn on to the four-track line at Huntington Drive en route to downtown Los Angeles. Note the street signs in this pre-freeway era. (Courtesy Metro Library.)

In this late 1940s photograph, a single Red Car leaves the Sixth and Main Streets elevated depot for Sierra Madre via a line that left the Huntington Drive right-of-way at San Marino and was mostly single-track. (Courtesy Jack Hedden/Jim Walker Collection.)

A "Portland Twelve" steel PE interurban heads west on Aliso Street at Alameda Street in the late 1940s. The Hollywood Freeway obliterated this corner. (Courtesy Jack Hedden/Jim Walker Collection.)

A three-car train of "Hollywood" cars in "Valley Seven" livery heads for Macy Street carhouse on January 2, 1939, after delivering a crowd for the Rose Parade. The parade and game were held on Monday, January 2, because neither event were ever held on a Sunday. (Courtesy Will Whittaker/Jim Walker Collection.)

A two-car train of "Hollywoods" heads west on the private right-of-way of the Venice Short Line in March 1939 toward the oceanfront community. They pass by the waiting station, called "Helms" for the Helms Bakery it served. Another icon in front of the station building was an Acme semaphore traffic signal. Speaking of icons, the statue of *The Helmsman* was also in the median of Venice Boulevard in front of the bakery (it has since been moved to Marina Del Rey). (Courtesy Metro Library.)

A southbound 100 Series steel car, built in 1930, pauses along Magnolia Avenue in Riverside County for its mandatory stop at the Union Pacific grade crossing on the local line from Riverside to Arlington in 1942. Rail service was converted to buses in 1943. (Courtesy Craig Rasmussen Collection.)

This photograph shows downtown Los Angeles in 1947. The photographer looks west on First at Los Angeles Streets to capture a two-car train of Ten Hundreds headed to Pasadena on the Short Line, which will go through South Pasadena on Fair Oaks Avenue. All the structures in this image are gone, replaced by city buildings and lawns. (Courtesy Craig Rasmussen Collection.)

Pacific Electric owned hundreds of buses made by White Motors. This is an official equipment portrait of a White at Torrance shops in 1952. (Courtesy Metro Library.)

From 1940 to 1943, PE cars detoured over the Macy Street Bridge, spanning the Los Angeles River near Union Station, while a new bridge was built on Aliso Street. PE cars ran over the new structure until 1951, when the tracks—and Red Cars—were evicted from the bridge and the interchange of the Ramona (now San Bernardino) and Santa Ana Parkways was opened. This 1943 view shows a Baldwin Park–bound car curving off Macy Street at the east end of its bridge and returning to the Aliso Street route. Completion of the freeway infrastructure in 1951 rang a death knell for the Red Cars that used this entrance into the central city, as PE did not contribute its share of construction costs. (Courtesy Craig Rasmussen Collection.)

This broadside view of an eastbound PE three-car train on the Macy Street Bridge was taken from the bottom of the Los Angeles River on March 6, 1941, at about where the Aliso Street replacement span was built. The PE traffic shared dual-gauge tracks with Los Angeles Railway on a detour from 1940 to 1943, while a new motor vehicle–electric railway span was built on the Aliso Street alignment. (Courtesy Will C. Whittaker/Jim Walker Collection.)

82

The interior waiting room, which was also used for ticket sales, information, lockers, and food service, of the PE Sixth and Main Streets depot was truly a beehive of activity when this photograph of the information desk was taken in the early 1940s. Above the desk hangs a star flag showing the number of PE employees who joined the military during World War II. (Courtesy Metro Library.)

A crowd awaits a Venice-bound Short Line train of wooden Red Cars at Vineyard in the 1940s. West Boulevard was the street atop a bridge that spanned the PE track laid in a ride-of-the-road private right-of-way next to Venice Boulevard. (Courtesy Metro Library.)

It's hard to believe that the Hollywood Freeway through Cahuenga Pass was ever this lightly used, but when the joint motor-vehicle-electric-railway stretch from Barham Boulevard to Highland Avenue opened in 1940, this scene was recorded on film. The PE line was abandoned in 1952, and what had been the center right-of-way later became two more lanes for motor-vehicle use. This photograph, looking toward Hollywood at the Mulholland Highway Bridge, was taken about 1941. (Courtesy Metro Library.)

When the massive viaduct taking the PE Venice Short Line over La Cienega Boulevard was completed in February 1930, the 2,300-foot structure cost $215,000 ($70,000 each shared by the City and County of Los Angeles and the balance by Pacific Electric). Despite PE having 68 grade separations, the many grade crossings with streets and the highway would be part of the undoing of the Red Cars. Here an eastbound trolley Railway Post Office Car has just gone over the thoroughfare on July 11, 1947. (Courtesy Craig Rasmussen Collection.)

Seen here in 1947 just outside the outer portal of PE's subway tunnel at First Street and Glendale Boulevard is Toluca Yard, where Red Cars were kept between runs. The yard opened as part of the subway facilities in 1925. Out of the picture at left is Toluca substation. The large bridge in the distance, constructed in 1942, carried First Street over Glendale Boulevard. First Street became Beverly Boulevard at this location. The yard was removed after the abandonment of the last PE subway rail line in 1955. (Courtesy Metro Library.)

This was the station yard for electric cars at the Calship Shipyard on Terminal Island. The shipyard, established in February 1941 before the beginning of World War II, turned out 467 vessels (called Liberty ships). The special Calship train brought employees (at its peak more than 282,000) to the big plant, which closed September 28, 1945. The last train ran to the island on September 15. (Courtesy Metro Library.)

When PE was converting many of its rail lines to bus operation in the 1930s, it bought many new pieces of rolling stock. This 14-seat coach from Yellow Coach (later folded into parent General Motors) came in 1941 and had a baggage compartment in the rear. It was a one-of-a-kind demonstrator that did not apparently result in a large order. It sits for its official portrait during the 1940s at the Sixth and Los Angeles Streets corner of PE's Sixth and Main Streets depot. The large office building behind the coach housed the local headquarters of the Santa Fe Railway, and the building at far right (only the corner is visible) was the Greyhound bus depot. (Courtesy Metro Library.)

In 1923, PE and Los Angeles Railway formed Los Angeles Motor Bus Company (LAMB), a joint operation, which changed to Motor Coach in 1928 because it was more "dignified." The companies did this to challenge a proposed "People's Motor Bus Company" promoted by Richard W. Meade and William Gibbs MacAdoo, who proposed buying 100 double-decker buses for a comprehensive network—if they won the election. The voters at a May 2 referendum, however, opted for the PE-LARy proposal to form LAMB, which became active August 1, 1923. LAMB's first route was on Western Avenue from Hollywood Boulevard to Slauson Avenue. The company was dissolved in 1949. Its owners divvied up its real estate and buses. By 1945, Los Angeles Railway had been replaced by Los Angeles Transit Lines, controlled by National City Lines, a Chicago-based transit operator. This early 1950s view was of Pacific Electric No. 2610 (once in the LAMC's 4500 series) at PE's West Hollywood facility. (Courtesy Metro Library.)

Seven

MORE BUSES, NEW COMPANY, AND THE END OF RED CARS

1951–1961

Big changes to the PE came during 1950 and 1951, when the Venice Short Line and all rail operations on the Northern District were converted to buses. Passenger rail operations were cut from Santa Ana to Bellflower without direct replacement, and the Newport Beach line was completely converted to buses.

In 1952, the San Fernando Valley rail line, which featured almost nine miles of freeway median line in Cahuenga Pass, was converted to bus operation. Resistance from the California Department of Highways to include rail transit in other freeway medians helped seal the early doom of passenger rail travel. In 1953, PE decided to rid itself of all remaining passenger services.

On October 1, 1953, rail and bus passenger operations were turned over to a new company, Metropolitan Coach Lines, which was intent upon quickly converting all remaining rail services to buses. Although MCL did succeed in converting the Beverly Hills–via–Hollywood and Glendale-Burbank operations to bus service and in ending the use of the PE subway, it failed to get rid of the five remaining Southern District rail services to and from Watts, Bellflower, Long Beach, San Pedro, and Catalina Dock.

The year 1956 saw the dieselization of freight operations, which had begun in 1943, except for a tiny operation in West Hollywood, which lasted until 1958. So the only electric rail service was the five remaining passenger lines, which PE was no longer operating. In 1958, Metropolitan Coach Lines (and Los Angeles Transit Lines, successor to the Los Angeles Railway) sold out to a public agency, the Los Angeles Metropolitan Transit Authority—the "first" MTA—which operated from 1951 to 1964. The first MTA had converted the remaining Southern District rail lines to buses by 1961. The Long Beach route (today's Metro Blue Line of the Los Angeles County Metropolitan Transportation Authority) was the last to go, on April 9, 1961.

The 1950s saw the conversion of more PE rail lines to bus operation. This March 18, 1951, view of an area just east of the Los Angeles River shows how PE would fit into grade separations east of the Aliso Street Bridge. But a few days later, Car No. 1113, headed for Monrovia and Glendora, was sold, along with the other 49 Eleven Hundreds, to the General Urquiza Railway in Buenos Aires, Argentina. Smaller Hollywood-type cars would handle the rail route until its demise on September 30, 1951. (Courtesy Metro Library.)

The dieselization of PE's freight was almost complete by 1956, the last year of electrics, except for an isolated operation in West Hollywood that kept going until 1958. This shot was taken at Graham Yard on the Southern District in 1956. Locomotive No. 1623 is switching cars, while diesel locomotive No. 1377 awaits its crew. The trolley pole mounted on the diesel was only used to trigger grade-crossing signals. Most of PE by then had been changed to rail circuitry for this function. (Courtesy Jim Walker.)

By 1952, all yard track was removed from Macy Street Yard, which was now a paved bus facility. The then unused track alongside awaited removal; the wires had already been pulled down. At this time, all of PE's Northern District was bus operated. (Courtesy Metro Library.)

One of the last conversions from rail to bus occurred after PE had sold its passenger service in 1953. The Glendale–Burbank line, equipped with 1940-built streamlined cars, went to bus operation on June 19, 1955. Here a two-car train of streamliners has just passed Alameda Street, as it gallops—the track had become very rough—toward its Burbank terminal in May 1951. (Courtesy Craig Rasmussen Collection.)

This typical 1950s view shows a PE blimp, the nickname affectionately given to the former Bay Area cars of enormous size, which were used in the last rail years. The train, en route to Bellflower, sits at the Lynwood station in 1955. (Courtesy Jim Walker.)

Crossing the Southern Pacific line at Dominguez (note the tower), a Red Car from Long Beach heads for Los Angeles in December 1955. The building in the left distance is the now-gone Dominguez substation. The tower has also disappeared, and 2006's Metro Blue Line is on a long bridge over the railroad and nearby highways. (Courtesy Craig Rasmussen Collection.)

In the early 1950s, a common sight in downtown Glendale on Brand Boulevard was a train of PE streamliners en route to downtown Los Angeles's subway terminal on Hill Street, stopping for passengers at Broadway. This was the last line to use the PE subway, and it was converted to buses (and the subway closed) in 1955. (Courtesy Metro Library.)

There were two smiling faces in this September 1953 photograph of Metropolitan Coach Lines president Jesse L. Haugh (left), who is handing a check to PE head Oscar A. Smith (right) to turn over rail and bus passenger service to MCL, effective October 1, 1953. Haugh's firm quickly took steps to convert PE's few remaining rail passenger services to bus, as promised in the deal. (Courtesy Metro Library.)

When PE was contemplating a changeover of its last remaining Northern District rail lines to bus operation, it had a sample bus built by its two largest suppliers. Car No. 2150 (above) was built by Twin Coach in 1949. It was the company's model 52-S2. It had 52 seats and was propelled by a gasoline engine, a Fageol Twin Coach–210 horsepower (FTC-210). The huge bus was tested in the spring of 1950. It is seen here at Macy Street Yard. The Truck and Coach Division built this Model No. 4510 bus (below) with 39 forward-facing seats in 1950. It had a diesel-fueled, 200-horsepower Model No. 671 engine. Both buses had automatic transmission. (Courtesy No. 2150 Metro Library, No. 2700 Gerald L. Squier.)

Shiny new GM-built 2900 Series PE diesels are displayed at the Van Nuys Yard in June 1953, with PE "brass," or bosses, standing in front of them. Another photograph in this book shows a cavalcade of them over Cahuenga Pass (p. 95) to that yard. (Courtesy Metro Library.)

Two of the last series of buses purchased by PE are seen in this night view in the Van Nuys Yard about 1952. (Courtesy Metro Library.)

Hollywood Boulevard was the main street of "Tinseltown" and was decorated for one of the Red Cars' final Yuletides in the 1950s (the line was converted to buses in September 1954). At right is the Warner's movie palace, displaying the original Cinerama program. At night, the Christmas Trees, lighted and attached to the streetlights, revolved. (Courtesy Metro Library.)

An important junction for PE's Southern District was at Watts, which was also the end of the four-track line. Here in 1953, a round-window blimp turns onto the Santa Ana route, but it only runs to Bellflower (freight-only service beyond that point). At left is the Watts Tower and the brick structure at right is substation No. 4, just below 103rd Street. (Courtesy Craig Rasmussen Collection.)

94

The PE Long Beach line was one of the biggest grossers of the system. This view of a Long Beach–bound Red Car shows it crossing the Los Angeles River on a double-track pile trestle dating back to the line beginnings. However, in 1956, at the behest of the Los Angeles County flood-control officials, this trestle was demolished and replaced with a steel-girder, single-track bridge with V-shaped concrete bents to prevent a buildup of debris from floods (of which the river had plenty). The single-track bridge was replaced by a double-track in the 1980s for the Metro Blue Line operation. (Courtesy Craig Rasmussen Collection.)

The summer after the conversion of the San Fernando Valley line from rail to bus in 1952, a line of new 2900-class (TDH-4801 model) GM buses create a "photo opportunity" as they go through Cahuenga Pass on the Hollywood Freeway. (Courtesy Metro Library.)

Months before the photograph on the previous page was taken, PE rails still had a place in the median of the Hollywood Freeway. This photograph looks east near Barham Boulevard. (Courtesy Metro Library.)

A southbound blimp Red Car crosses the Los Angeles River just north of the Los Cerritos stop in a ritzy portion of Long Beach in the 1950s. This single track was replaced by a double-track bridge in the late 1980s for the Metro Blue Line. (Courtesy Metro Library.)

The inside of a "Hollywood" car is shown here in the 1950s. The seats were reversible (they rotated) and were upholstered in zebra-stripe mohair. The contraption in the middle of the car held the fare box, used when a two-man operation was needed. (Courtesy Metro Library.)

The inside of one of PE's blimp interurbans shows the reversible seats upholstered in a less vivid patterned mohair. (Courtesy Metro Library.)

The trestle over a gap in the hills on the new Glendale line was built for the new electric railway line in 1904, but agitation to build Fletcher Drive through the gap caused the removal of the center portion of the timber and the installation of steel girders that gave a 40-foot, 9-inch clearance from the pavement. The modification was completed in 1928. The structure was razed in 1959 after the rail line was removed. (Courtesy Metro Library.)

Riders leaving the Los Angeles County Fair at Pomona in October 1951 wait at gate nine for special coaches to Pomona. By this time, buses had replaced special trains to the fair. (Courtesy Metro Library.)

The station at North Hollywood was a joint Pacific Electric–Southern Pacific agency that served PE's San Fernando Valley rail line. After passenger service on the Valley line switched to buses in 1952, the wooden structure was rented out for various uses, including a lumber yard. The now-bedraggled structure still exists at the same location, but the right-of-way has become a busway. (Courtesy Metro Library.)

In 1929, one of the interurban cars bought from the recently abandoned suburban-electric lines out of Portland, Oregon, by PE was run through Torrance shops, emerging as Officers' Car No. 1299. It had a lounge section at each end, with a bathroom and kitchen in the middle. It was usually used on inspection trips, but often was used by rail enthusiasts for excursions. The car was retired in 1958 and is now at the Orange Empire Railway Museum in Perris, California. (Courtesy Jim Walker.)

A 1940s view of the ramp from San Pedro Street into PE's Main Street station in Los Angeles shows two "Hollywood" cars: one leaving the depot and one arriving. (Courtesy Metro Library.)

A 1952 image from the elevated rail station looks north on Los Angeles Street, as a PE bus awaits the light to change at Sixth Street. At right is the Greyhound bus depot. (Courtesy Metro Library.)

A "Hollywood" car sits on the westbound track on Hollywood Boulevard and Highland Avenue. It is en route to Beverly Hills on the Beverly Hills–via–Hollywood Boulevard route in about 1952. The cross track is for the San Fernando Valley line, which went north on Highland to center median track through Cahuenga Pass in the center of the Hollywood Freeway. (Courtesy Metro Library.)

After 1950, passenger service on PE's line from Los Angeles to Santa Ana was cut back to Bellflower. Here an outbound blimp car to Bellflower pulls into the Lynwood station at Long Beach Boulevard in 1953. (Courtesy Jim Walker.)

A southbound PE car climbs up the grade to the bridge that spanned Firestone Boulevard. Among the functions of the tall poles was to support the trolley wire and carry power from a nearby substation to feed, periodically, the overhead wires. They also carried lines for communication and control. (Courtesy Metro Library.)

A common sight on the Pacific Electric in later years was a diesel locomotive–powered freight train. Lack of a trolley pole on the locomotive would indicate circuitry for grade-crossing signals in Lynwood, where this photograph was taken about 1957, has been changed to the track. (Courtesy Jim Walker.)

Eight

PE's Last Years
1961–1965

Some of the rail lines, those that did not have freight potential or faced local opposition to freight trains in streets, were simply torn up, and all or portions of others continued, even to the present.

The Pacific Electric ceased to exist as an entity on August 13, 1965, and its remains—45 locomotives and about 210 miles of lines—were folded into parent company Southern Pacific. SP itself ceased to exist on September 11, 1996, after it merged into Union Pacific Railroad.

The passenger-hauling function of PE ceased in 1953, when that operation was sold. PE then became a low-speed switching road, using a small portion of its once-mighty rail network throughout the Los Angeles basin. Only a few buildings or lines remind people of a glorious period of the Red Car empire.

One telltale sign that a piece of track was once part of the PE system when it was electrified is a traction-bonded joint between rail sections. Similar, smaller bonds are sometimes used for signal circuits. The purpose of a traction bond was to ensure good ground return to complete an electric circuit. (Courtesy Jim Walker.)

The post-passenger years on the PE were melancholy because the line became a shell its former self. This view looks south at the Slauson Tower, the crossing of the Santa Fe's Harbor subdivision. It depicts how the once-mighty four-track stem had been whittled down to a single-track diamond (crossing) to save maintenance costs. (Courtesy Jim Walker Collection.)

Devoid of wire, diesel locomotive No. 1005 visits Watts Tower (left) in 1962. The track, still in place at Watts Junction, had not yet been "rationalized," or reduced, to fit freight-only needs. (Courtesy Jim Walker Collection.)

This photograph is of what had been one of PE electrified lines' fairly standard grade crossings. It had a "wig-wag" warning signal mounted on a pole and a white "crossbuck" on the other side of the road. These installations were generally grandfathered in until the grade crossing was changed, usually when the road was widened, at which point flasher lights—and sometimes gates at busier crossings—were mandated. (Courtesy Jim Walker Collection.)

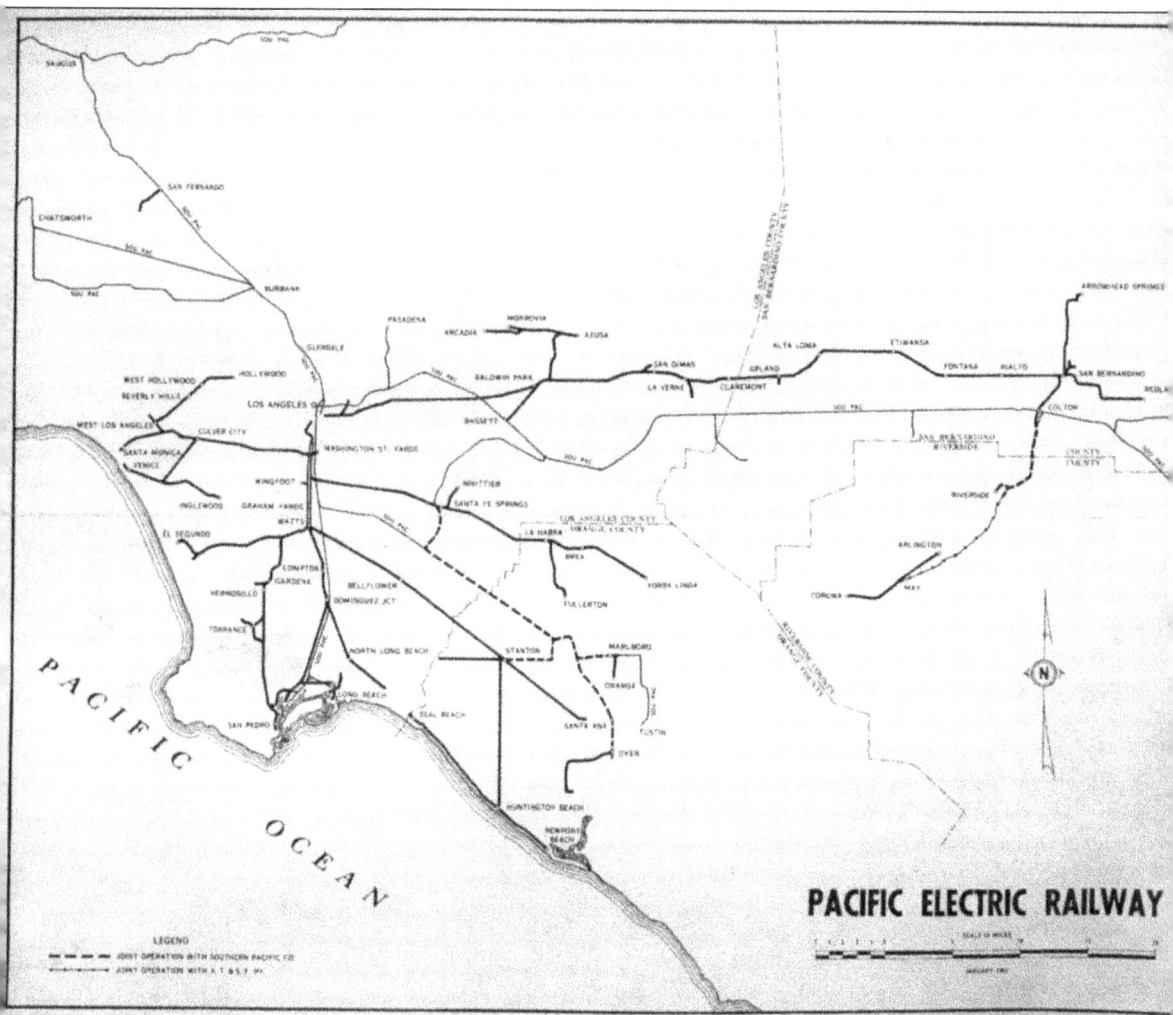

The remains of the "world's greatest electric railway system" are seen in this early 1960s map of Pacific Electric that appeared on an employee timetable. Many lines had been torn up, and PE had to use trackage rights on other railroads to reach some of its now-isolated lines. (Courtesy Jim Walker Collection.)

Nine

POSTLUDE AND GALLERY

In the 21st century, PE is just a memory and few people who actually rode the Red Cars are still alive. But rail transit is not dead in and around Los Angeles. The present public agency, Los Angeles County Metropolitan Transportation Authority, is now operating one heavy-rail rapid-transit line, the Metro Red Line (all in subway), and light-rail lines (Metro Blue, Green, and Gold). Construction is under way on the Eastside Gold Line extension and the Expo light-rail line, and extension of the Gold Line deeper into the San Gabriel Valley is being considered. Plans for further extensions and new rail lines are being mooted. In addition, there are Metrolink locomotive-hauled commuter trains to such destinations as Oxnard, Lancaster, San Bernardino, Riverside, various Orange County points, and Oceanside. Rail travel is increasing in this era of street gridlock and provides logistically and economically sound cargo movement.

Presented here are samplings of PE's myriad services at various times and places. In this small book, there is no possibility of showing every aspect of activity on the Red Car system.

Watts Junction was a big part of PE's Southern District lines. The Santa Ana, El Segundo, and other Southwest cities' lines parted here, and the Long Beach, San Pedro, and Newport lines kept going toward the coast. This metal building was Watts carhouse, which was used to service the local line that ended here (two "Hollywood" cars are shown in the yard). Mechanical crews also service locomotives here. There were fewer electrics by the mid–20th century and more and more diesels as the years passed. Not in this c. 1940 view are the office and crew rooms added in later years. (Courtesy Metro Library.)

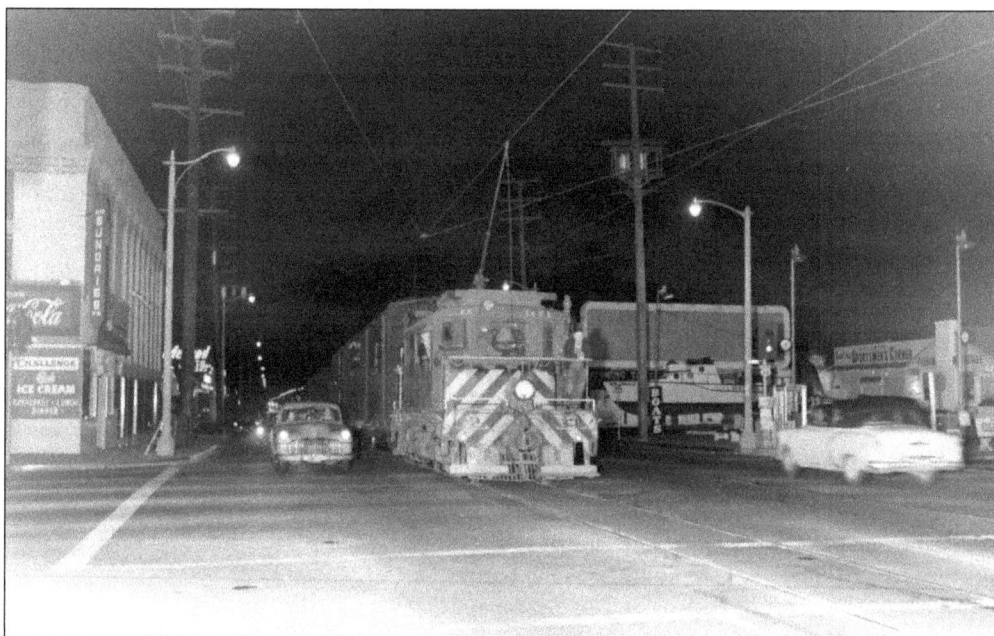

A nocturnal visitor to Santa Monica Boulevard in Hollywood is PE electric locomotive No. 1624, switching at the corner of La Brea Avenue in 1957. After all the rest of PE's freight operation was dieselized in 1957, this "island" of electric operation remained from the West Hollywood shops east on Santa Monica to Seward Street in Hollywood. It was dieselized (wire taken down) in January 1958. (Courtesy Craig Rasmussen Collection.)

One of the last freight yards to be switched by electrics was Graham Yard, located at Ninety-second Street, and the four-track Southern District main stem, just south of Firestone Boulevard. Here is "Juice Jack," locomotive No. 1626, at work. (Courtesy Jim Walker.)

Valley Junction was where the Pasadena Short Line, Pasadena Oak Knoll, Sierra Vista Local, Sierra Madre, and Glendora-Monrovia routes split off from the main trunk line to San Bernardino. A PE "steeple cab" pulls a train of refrigerated freight cars, often called "Reefers," and is seen in front of Valley Junction substation in the early 1930s. Line voltage in the trolley wire on the San Bernardino line rose from 600 volts direct current to 1,200 volts direct current east of this point. (Courtesy Metro Library.)

During World War II, PE leased steam locomotives from other roads on the Southern Pacific, such as the San Diego and Arizona 27, a 4-6-0 (a two-axle pilot truck, three axles of drivers, and no trailing truck) seen here with electric locomotive No. 1630 at La Verne in 1944. The steam locomotive was built by the Baldwin Locomotive Works in 1919 and went to scrap in December 1949.

Steam locomotives on an electric railway? Yes, many were owned by or leased to PE from 1922 to the late 1940s. Locomotive No. 1506 is shown here switching cars at Dolores Yard, not far south of Dominguez Junction on the Los Angeles–San Pedro–via–Dominguez line in 1943. The steamers augmented PE's fleet of electric locomotives and PE No. 1506 (nee parent Southern Pacific's S-8 class 0-6-0 No. 1123) was scrapped in November 1949. (Courtesy Craig Rasmussen Collection.)

Equipped with poles to actuate grade-crossing protection and signals still circuited through trolley wire, diesel locomotive No. 4603, leased from parent Southern Pacific, is seen in May 1956 at Graham Yard. By then, most of the PE freight trains were pulled with diesel locomotives. (Courtesy Jim Walker.)

A pair of center-cab General Electric 44-ton diesels, Nos. 1650 and 1651, began the diesel era on PE in 1943. They were equipped with trolley poles only to trip overhead wire circuits for grade-crossing protection (later these were track-circuited, obviating the need for poles and trolley wire). Pictured here in the 1940s is No. 1651; it was leased to SP in 1954. (Courtesy Craig Rasmussen Collection.)

The largest diesel locomotives to carry the PE name on their flanks were the 5200 Series, some of which were even equipped with trolley poles to trigger grade-crossing protection. No. 5241 heads a westbound PE freight at the crossing of the SP main line at El Monte in April 1951. The 1,500-horsepower units were built by Baldwin Locomotive Works for SP, and some were leased to PE. They immediately disclosed a big problem: size. The units couldn't make all the tight turns on PE, and they were too heavy for most PE spurs. So a few years later they were returned to SP and replaced by lighter motive power units that could take tight curves. (Courtesy Craig Rasmussen Collection.)

One of PE's sources of revenue was Railway Express packages carried on express cars, or "box motors." These self-propelled freight cars ran on routes and schedules like those of passenger trains. Here packages are transferred from electric car to a local agent's truck. (Courtesy Craig Rasmussen Collection.)

A big collection point for packages was at the street level of the Sixth and Main Streets depot. Here a Railway Express Agency truck is being loaded with packages brought in by PE for local delivery about 1950. On the north side of Sixth Street, across from the PE complex, is Los Angeles's Greyhound bus depot. (Courtesy Metro Library.)

A big terminal for express packages was at Los Angeles Union passenger terminal, which opened in 1939. This portion of the facility was built for PE's box motors. This photograph dates from the 1940s. When the Northern District of PE was converted to buses in 1951, access to the passenger terminal was broken, and PE got out of the express business altogether in 1952. (Courtesy Craig Rasmussen Collection.)

PE's Monrovia-Glendora line crosses the Santa Fe's Second District at Arcadia. The tower, built in 1919 to replace a 1904 facility (the latter was damaged in a 1911 derailment), was staffed by Santa Fe employees and demolished in 1954 after the PE line was abandoned. Railway Post Office Car No. 1406 heads east. (Courtesy Craig Rasmussen Collection.)

Downtown Long Beach once had a PE carhouse, on the east side of American Avenue (now Long Beach Boulevard) at Fifth Street. In this 1919 view, an express motor is ready for its journey north on the wide thoroughfare. In 1930, the carbarn, substation, and associated buildings were replaced by a new facility called Fairbanks Avenue Yard at the end of Seventh Street, on the east bank of the Los Angeles River. One item in the new complex forecasts the future: a motorbus garage. (Courtesy Metro Library.)

114

Railway Post Office (RPO) Car No. 1405 is seen here about 1950 at Macy Street Yard. The RPOs were box motors specially equipped for security; the clerks aboard worked for the post office and were armed with pistols. They had fixed routes, and PE provided this service from 1905 to 1950. The remaining RPOs were then stripped of their federally mandated equipment and returned into ordinary box-motor internal configuration. (Courtesy Craig Rasmussen Collection.)

The 800 Series had been a mainstay of PE from its earliest years, but by the end of the 1930s, most had been sent to the junkyard. However, five of the series were slightly rebuilt into box motors 1495–1499 (they retained seats, but a center door was cut in midships) in 1940. Then came World War II, and the five were returned to their passenger numbers and served as the Torrance-shop train in 1942, 1943, and part of 1944, at which time they resumed their careers as box motors 1495–1499. This car is seen at the Torrance shops during World War II, and it would be scrapped in 1951 as box motor Car No. 1496. (Courtesy Metro Library.)

Box motor Car No. 1457 is westbound on a long trestle over the San Gabriel River west of Baldwin Park in November 1943. It was built in 1913 as a passenger motor for the SP Red Electric suburban out of Portland, Oregon. That system was abandoned in 1920s, done in by automobiles, and most of the rolling stock was sold to PE in 1928. Two of the "Portlands" were pulled out of storage in 1937 and rebuilt into box motors; this one became PE 1457. It was scrapped in 1954. (Courtesy Jim Walker Collection.)

Box motor 1461 turns south from Sixth Street onto Hill Street in the 1940s. It was once a passenger car on an interurban railway out of Portland, Oregon, before coming to the PE. Shop forces did a "quick and dirty" conversion to hauling less-than-carload (LCLO) freight, leaving in the outline of windows while cutting in two side doors. (Courtesy Metro Library.)

This was the shops and storage yard of Pacific Electric at West Hollywood as seen in 1950. It was built for the Los Angeles Pacific interurban, a PE predecessor, and the complex and surrounding area was once called Sherman. Note the large brick building that served as shops. All this is gone now, and the site is now used for a bus division and the Pacific Design Center, the "Blue Whale." (Courtesy Metro Library.)

A view of Macy Street Yard and shops, seen from a hillside to the southeast, was captured on film in 1951, the last year the Pacific Electric had a rail presence at the complex. Ramona Boulevard, in the foreground, is now the San Bernardino Freeway (Interstate 10). (Courtesy Metro Library.)

An impressive brick and steel carhouse was built at San Bernardino in 1915. It is seen in 1924 with an array of PE interurban cars, locomotives, local streetcars, and—yes—a bus. Unfortunately, a fire struck the structure in the 1980s, and its remains were razed. (Courtesy Metro Library.)

The largest presence of the PE in its Northern District was this carhouse and the shops at Macy Street Yard, which also included a large outdoor yard. The first facilities there were built in 1917, and its shop was next in size to the main system shops at Torrance. This is the carhouse in 1941. Bus use of the yard dates to 1941, and the last railcar usage at the location was in 1951. The site is used in the 21st century as a bus yard, the LACMTA Division 10. (Courtesy Craig Rasmussen Collection.)

This is a 1924 aerial view of PE's vast Torrance shops, built on a 125-acre site in the South Bay. The Torrance shops' property was purchased in 1915, and by November 1919, the facility was completed, although portions of it were rushed into service before. Many cars were heavily rebuilt there and some pieces of railway power and other railway vehicles were turned out. This large facility replaced the now-cramped shops at Seventh and Alameda Streets in Los Angeles as PE approached its zenith in the 1920s. The Torrance shops closed on May 16, 1955. (Courtesy Metro Library.)

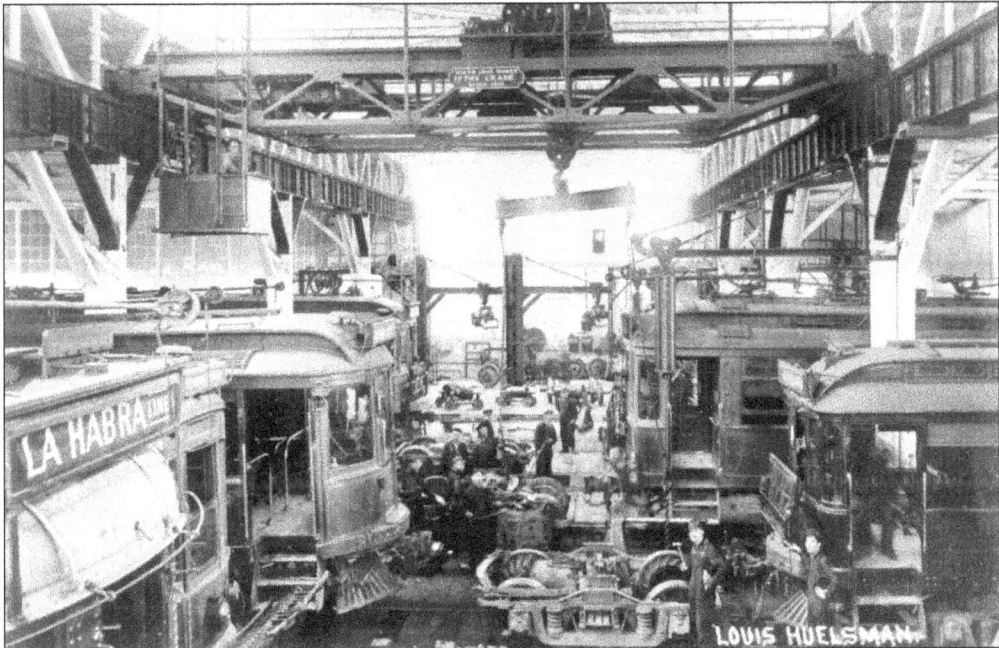

One of the many interior bays of Torrance shops is seen in this early view of the hustle and bustle that prevailed in the 1920s. (Courtesy Metro Library.)

Seen from its southern end in the 1950s, the Watts carhouse serviced Watts Local Line "Hollywood" cars and freight locomotives. It was about a long block south of 103rd Street, just south of the Watts Tower. (Courtesy Metro Library.)

Three Red Cars are seen at the Pasadena carhouse on North Fair Oaks Avenue in the second block north of Colorado Street in 1927. The carhouse also opened into Raymond Avenue. A 1970 earthquake caused heavy damage, a sure reason for demolition, which happened soon after. (Courtesy Craig Rasmussen Collection.)

The Hill Street surface station, on the west side of street between Fourth and Fifth Streets, was built in 1908 by PE predecessor Los Angeles Pacific. When the Subway Terminal building was opened, waiting room space was moved to the new structure. Surface lines continued to operate even after some PE lines to the west had moved to the new subway in 1926. (Courtesy Metro Library.)

The elevated terminal and surface terminal at the Sixth and Main Streets depot are shown in this 1920s view, looking northwest. The building at left (out of view) is the Pacific Electric station and offices. (Courtesy Craig Rasmussen Collection.)

The elevated station behind the Sixth and Main Streets PE depot was a dramatic setting for photographs. Here is a late 1930s view of a three-car train of Ten Hundreds on the Alhambra–San Gabriel–Temple City line, just arriving up the viaduct from San Pedro Street to the elevated platform. (Courtesy Metro Library.)

After conversion of the Venice Short Line to buses on September 15, 1950, what had been a private right-of-way called the Trolleyway (black strip at left) became a street called Neilson Way. New buildings were erected for a bus division (now Division Six). A vestige of electric railway (the brick building at right) was the Ocean Park substation. At far right is another example of "industrial archeology"—a gasholder. Both the building and gasholder are gone.

One of the impressive features of PE's Sixth and Main Streets headquarters building and station was this concourse through the structure. This night view, looking east from Main Street, was taken long after rail service had been converted to buses. (Courtesy Jim Walker.)

In the heart of the San Fernando Valley was substation No. 31 Van Nuys, housed in this concrete building. There was also one other substation in the valley, North Hollywood, on Vineland. A proposed third sub, to be named "Wheeler," was never built. (Courtesy Metro Library.)

This is the North Long Beach substation at Willow Street and American Avenue in 1956. It had a portable substation unit on an adjoining siding. The curved track without overhead wires in the foreground is now the freight-only Newport Beach line. This substation was feeding power to the Los Angeles–Long Beach line, last of the Red Car routes. (Courtesy Jim Walker.)

To augment a substation installation (or to replace it when it is down for repairs), the PE had many portable substations (on wheels) that could be towed to a siding alongside the building. Portable substations might also be set up for special events (like the Rose Parade in Pasadena) for unusually heavy power needs. Here is one of the portable substations being towed to an outlying substation by diesel–electric Car No. 1654, equipped with trolley poles to actuate grade-crossing protection. (Courtesy Craig Rasmussen.)

Typical of the design and appearance of many other such installations on the PE was the San Pedro substation, north of the port city of the same name. Built in 1920, the brick structure served Red Cars to San Pedro until the rail service from Los Angeles to San Pedro was converted to buses, on December 7, 1958. (Courtesy Metro Library.)

Maintenance and repair of the electrical system was vital on the Red Car system. Here tower Car No. 1731 and crew are at work in the 1920s. This type of overhead wire was called catenary. (Courtesy Craig Rasmussen Collection.)

A sad image, but its the end for PE cars in this view at a Terminal Island (between Long Beach and San Pedro) scrap yard in the 1950s. Most of the Red Cars had lasted way beyond what they were built for, a tribute to rail transportation. (Courtesy Metro Library.)

BIBLIOGRAPHY

Bail, Eli. *From Railway to Freeway, Pacific Electric and the Motor Coach*. Glendale, CA: Interurban Press, 1984.

Crump, Spencer. *Ride the Big Red Cars*. Glendale, CA: Interurban Press, 1988.

Duke, Donald. *Pacific Electric Railway* (four volumes: Southern, Western, Northern, Eastern Districts). San Marino, CA: Golden West Books, 2002–2004.

Electric Railway Association of Southern California. *Pacific Electric Stations*. Los Angeles: 1998.

Orange Empire Railway Museum. *Pacific Electric Corporate History 1885–1911*. Perris, CA: 1998.

Orange Empire Railway Museum. *The Life and Times of the Pacific Electric*. Perris, CA: 1983.

Robinson, John W. *The San Gabriels: Southern California Mountain Country*. San Marino, CA: Golden West Books, 1977.

Swett, Ira L. *Tractions of the Orange Empire Special 41*. Los Angeles: Interurban, 1967.

————. *Lines of Pacific Electric* (two volumes: Special 60, Southern and Western Districts, Special 61, Northern and Eastern Districts). Glendale, Calif.: Interurban Press, 1975-1976.

————. *Cars of Pacific Electric* (three volumes: 28–City and Suburban; 36–Interurban and Deluxe; 37–Combos, Locomotives and Non-Revenue Cars) Glendale, CA: Interurban Press, 1975, 1976, 1978.

————. *Pacific Electric Album of Cars–Interurbans Special 39*. Los Angeles: Interurbans, 1965.

Veysey, Laurence R. *Passenger Service of Pacific Electric–Interurban Special 21*. Los Angeles: Interurbans, 1958.

Visit us at
arcadiapublishing.com

www.ingramcontent.com/pod-product-compliance
Lightning Source LLC
Chambersburg PA
CBHW050712110426
42813CB00007B/2164